I0428489

Living on the Land: "The Earth Itself to Nobody"

CARLA M PATON

CARLA PATON

Copyright © 2014 Carla M Paton

All rights reserved.

ISBN-13:978-1503225480
ISBN-10:1503225488

Dedication

Dedicated to my husband, Kenneth B. Paton, and his

passionate Scottish, animal nature.

Table of Contents

Preface

This essay is a follow up to my earlier book on life on our ranch, *Engaging the Soul of the Great Plains and the Smoky Hill Trail*. In this present installment, I will be exploring the behavior of fencing and property ownership using James Hillman's idea of psychologizing, as well as his other moves or methods of personifying, pathologizing, and dehumanizing, as outlined in his seminal 1975 work, *Re-Visioning Psychology*.

"How can you buy or sell the sky—the warmth of the land?
The idea is strange to us. We do not own the freshness of
the air or the sparkle of the water. How can you buy them
from us?"

— Duwamish chief Sealth (qtd. in *Turtle Island Alphabet*)

"The first man who had fenced in a piece of land, said
'This is mine,' and found people naïve enough to believe
him, that man was the true founder of civil society. From
how many crimes, wars, and murders, from how many
horrors and misfortunes might not any one have saved
mankind, by pulling up the stakes, or filling up the ditch,
and crying to his fellows: Beware of listening to this
impostor; you are undone if you once forget that the fruits
of the earth belong to us all, and the earth itself to nobody."

— Jean-Jacques Rousseau, *Discourse on Inequality*

Fences

I think often these days of fences. On our 70 acres of property on the Eastern Plains of Colorado, we have a simple four-strand barbed wire fence that surrounds our land and separates it from our neighboring ranchers. That fencing is again "cross-fenced" into smaller internal areas designed to move cattle from and to different grazing zones. There is also a smaller fenced area of about an acre that surrounds the house designed to keep the dogs (two) from straying too far afield. This smaller fenced area has a manual gate that must be religiously opened and closed when leaving the house grounds with a vehicle or on foot. The larger outer fence has an automatic gate with a code and a security camera designed to keep out intruders. The interior manual gate however has been especially on my mind because when coming home to unload groceries, I have forgotten to close it three times. The last time, an unfortunate porcupine wandered into the backyard and was promptly eaten whole by our Siberian Huskie who had not yet been instructed in the way of sharp quills. (A lesson our smarter Japanese Akita had already learned—she did not *eat* the porcupine.) After eating said porcupine, our huskie (aptly named, Loki, the Norse god of mischief) then wandered out the gate to explore the wider world and to sniff out more tasty game.

Fences of course imply property and the concept and law of land ownership. This behavior of owning land and erecting fences to protect it in turn presumes that humans can "own"

a part of the earth, that we can entrap nature and call it "ours," and that it can belong to any one, or group of people, and not the whole, or simply not be owned at all. If we look behind the veil of this fencing and property ownership behavior, we can "see through" or do what Hillman (1975) described as *psychologizing* which allows the soul to "reflect upon its nature, structure, and purpose" (p. 117). In a further elaboration of psychologizing, Hillman (1975) said:

> *Psychologizing goes on whenever reflection takes place in terms other than those presented.* Is suspects an interior, not evident intention; it searches for a hidden clockwork, a ghost in the machine, an etymological root, something more than meets the eye; or it sees with another eye. It goes on whenever we move to a deeper level. (p. 134-135)

With this essay, I will be looking through to this "deeper level" and exploring the behavior of fencing and property ownership using Hillman's idea of psychologizing, as well as his other moves or methods of personifying, pathologizing, and dehumanizing, as outlined in his 1975 work, *Re-Visioning Psychology*.

The Great Promise

"The Nation behaves well if it treats the natural resources as assets which it must turn over to the next generation increased and not impaired in value; and behaves badly if it leaves the land poorer to those who come after it. That is what I mean by the phrase, conservation of natural resources. Use them; but use them so that as far as possible our children will be richer, and not poorer because we have lived."

—Theodore Roosevelt, *The New Nationalism* 52, 1910

Our 70acres was once part of a larger 8000 acre tract homesteaded in the 1800's by German immigrants whose descendants still live adjacent to us. Having always lived in the suburbs prior to our move to the country, I have learned a few lessons. The first time I drove the country dirt road to our house at night, I had to slam on my truck brakes to avoid hitting four cattle at once who were lying in the middle of the road. Unbeknownst to me (a "city girl") I had crossed a cattle guard and was in "open range." I was aware that I had crossed the cattle guard of course, but knew nothing of their greater meaning. My husband later found great mirth in informing me that in the land between two cattle guards; the cattle roam free, without the normal fencing along the road side. Henceforth, I have become much more conscious of fences and cattle. Not to mention the deer, antelope, coyotes, and occasional flock of wild turkeys. Driving at night is an especially perilous adventure.

The Homestead Act of 1862 opened the American West to settlers who were given 160 acre plots in return for residing on the land for five years, cultivating portions of it and paying the filing fees. Other homestead laws soon followed such as the Desert Lands Act of 1877 and the Stock-Raising Homestead Act of 1916 (Klein, Cheever, & Birdsong, 2005). These acts were the enablers of the hope of *Manifest Destiny* and the great myth of progress.

According to Fromm (2003):

> The Great Promise of Unlimited Progress [was] the
>
> promise of domination of nature, of material
>
> abundance, of the greatest happiness for the greatest
>
> number, and of unimpeded personal freedom. .
>
> .With industrial progress, from the substitution of
>
> mechanical and then nuclear energy for animal and
>
> human energy to the substitution of the computer
>
> for the human mind, we could feel that we were on
>
> our way to unlimited production and, hence,
>
> unlimited consumption. . .[and] the trinity of
>
> unlimited production, absolute freedom, and
>
> unrestricted happiness formed the nucleus of a new
>
> religion, Progress. (qtd. in, Kassiola, 2003, p. 29)

Additionally, Hillman (1971) considered progress to be a

monotheistic principle that had hierarchical stages that

were antithetical to the psyche and which had religious

13

overtones. He believed that instead, the psyche had "non-growth, non-upward and non-ordered components" and that with more room given for variance we might be more aligned to psyche' natural way of functioning (pp. 198-199).

Through the myths of Manifest Destiny and progress, we can psychologize or see through to the basic assumptions that are infrequently examined. The American colonists consisted mainly of European settlers who came from cramped and polluted industrial cities. With them, they brought both economic imperialism and a Romantic yearning for a return to an Eden pastoral landscape and lifestyle. Further, and perhaps more insidious, came the assumption that nature (and land) can be owned. With this ownership mindset also comes the hubris that nature is at the mercy of the owner to be regarded and used as resource for whatever may be the needs of the day.

Coupled with the myth of progress and a pastoral longing, was the support of science and technology. The rational science of physics and Darwin; of ordering, classifying, and naming gave and gives the illusion that science can reveal the true and only nature of nature. According to Mclaughlin (2003) this nature is a "lifeless matter in motion" that serves as a nothing more than resources (p. 106). The other assumption that comes with the provision of science is that we are able to control nature. This idea also presumes that we are not a part of nature; that we are instead outsiders manipulating an experiment; that we are objective Faustian operators who will reap the bounty of our supreme knowledge. These myths leave "nothing in our understanding of nature that places cultural barriers to the exploitation of nature. We have collectively lost any sense of the sacred in the natural world. Even the depth of this loss of the sacred is often unnoticed" (McLaughlin, 2003, p. 106).

As for the cattle and the fences, we have contained the chaos of the land. Where immune hardy, disease resistant native buffalo once roamed free and wide in the millions, we have decimated a species and the indigenous people who honored its essence and presence. We have instead crowded the public and private lands with overgrazing cattle that need antibiotics and hormones to resist all manner of infections that threaten their young, weak immune systems. Buffalo or American bison are also not sympathetic to weak cattle fencing. They are mighty, huge, strong, and wild. They will as soon follow their muzzles into the next rancher's land as stay in their own designated pasture. The cattle barbed wire is perfect for scratching their tough hides. A different breed of taller and sturdier fencing is in order for bison, but here, we are not speaking of purely wild animals, but those semi-domesticated as resources, for consumption.

The Fantasy

"You run like a herd of luminous deer

and I am dark, I am forest.

You are a wheel at which I stand,

whose dark spokes sometimes catch me up,

revolve me nearer to the center."

—Rilke, *The Book of Hours*

Psychologically, a fence acts like ego protection. The fence is a de-fense, a persona, a container. It is conscious of what is on the inside and what is out. It is meant to define and announce boundaries. It stands silent and still, but speaks loudly for the land owner even in the owner's absence. A fence assumes a "we" and a "them" an "inside" and an "outside." It acts as a maternal possession. All things inside the fence belong to the motherland, those outside, are children of a different mother, not our concern, not our problem. Raise them as you will, the fence says, I only have authority over my own stuff; I only have responsibility for that within my own confines. Nature however does not understand lawful boundaries.

Deer are particularly indifferent to fences. A small herd of mule deer roam our property. They leap over the short barbed wire fences with ease. Our grass and alfalfa hay is as good as the neighbors. Unlike the cattle, they are indeed wild creatures. Like psyche, like soul the deer are autonomous, unpredictable beings, that take flight like a startled dream, or which bed down when there is safe space for a deepening connection; an Eros of earth. These deer remind us of the "imaginative possibility in our natures." In speaking of soul, Hillman (1975) said:

First, 'soul' refers to the *deepening* of events into experiences; second, the significance soul makes possible, whether in love or in religious concern, derives from its special *relation with death*. And third, by 'soul' I mean the imaginative possibility in our natures, the experiencing through reflective

speculation, dream, image, and *fantasy*—that mode
which recognizes all realities as primarily symbolic
or metaphorical. (p. xvi)

One morning, at dawn, I gazed out on our front yard
and saw the small herd grazing. There were still adolescent
deer staying with their mothers. I looked away for a
moment to make tea and later turned back to see our huskie
on top of one of the small deer at the interior fence line. I
rushed outside screaming at the dogs to back away from the
young male who lay at an awkward angle against a fence
post. I could detect no blood, but after some time
determined that the dog, having run down the hill at top
speed, had run into the animal, slamming it into the post
and breaking its neck. I had never been with an animal as it
was dying, let alone such a creature of beauty and
perfection. He had been too small and too slow to leap over
the fence as his family had who still stood by outside the
fence, waiting on their brother. I watched with anguish as

they one by one disappeared into the trees; leaving their fallen comrade. I stroked and covered the small buck with a blanket; completely helpless to save its life. For the first time, I felt the powerlessness of my ego where nature is concerned. No phone call to the vet, no 911, no miracle cure of science to mend a broken neck; only the buck's pitiful cries and my own weeping as I leaned against the fence post, the dying deer in my arms.

The deer know no property lines, they know no ownership. They know only the earth as it always had been; open, expansive, gentle, and fierce. Yet the land shrinks, is fenced and fragmented, is desolated, is owned, is bought

and sold without a care for soul, or the imagination

roaming free. To imagine the fence as ego or the deer as

soul is to employ Hillman's (1975) move of personifying or

imagining things. "*Personifying* [is] to signify the basic

psychological activity—*the spontaneous experiencing,*

envisioning and speaking of the configurations of existence

of psychic presences" (p. 12). The deer to psyche are

images and a sensuous "connection with fantasy. To be in

soul is to experience the fantasy in all realities and the basic

reality of fantasy" (p. 23). According to Abraham (1998)

the deer's graceful caution, elegant leaps, sudden

appearances and swift vanishings link it to the alchemical

Mercurius, the transformative intermediary soul substance,

as well as to pilgrimage or initiation paths that are

circuitous, indirect, constantly shifting direction or, like the

deer, disappear altogether.

The Tragedy

"The outstanding scientific discovery of the twentieth century is not television, or radio, but rather the complexity of the land organism. Only those who know the most about it can appreciate how little is known about it....If the biota, in the course of aeons, has built something we like but do not understand, then who but a fool would discard seemingly useless parts? To keep every cog and wheel is the first precaution of intelligent tinkering."
—Aldo Leopold, *Essays on Conservation from Round River*, 1953

The idea of land ownership and its requisite fencing implies an established order and more to the point maintaining ownership. Property is bought and sold with the aid of good credit, banks, contracts, and laws. Hillman (2005) called such an authoritative system a *Senex* structure. Survey lines are marked and recorded. Boundary lines are fixed in space. Fence posts are stuck in the ground, cemented in place. Keys are handed over at a ritual "closing." There is finality to one's name on a deed and a grip of responsibility that execrably weaves one into the matrix of the economic system. According to Slater (2005):

> *Senex* and *puer* are Latin terms for 'old man' and 'young man,' and personify the poles of tradition, stasis, structure, and authority on one side, and immediacy, wandering, invention and idealism on the other. The senex consolidates, grounds and disciplines, the puer flashes with insight and thrives on fantasy and creativity. These diverging, conflicting tendencies are ultimately interdependent, forming two faces of the one configuration, each face never far from the other. 'Old' and 'new' maybe the most direct terms for the pair. They represent two very different ways of entering the world, but are oddly dependent on one another. (p. x)

From the viewpoint of the land, this senex perspective speaks of grounding. One is tied to a place. One puts down roots; remains fixed in place. A nest is built from which the young, the puer fly. This rootedness can be a positive boon for the earth. With a strong connection to a place, a fondness and appreciation is nurtured. With stillness and time, one can come to know the history and needs of land that requires remembrance and tending. The erosion of forgetfulness and apathy can be stanched. However, a stasis can also mean being stuck in ways which may need modification. Traditions may need the spark of new knowledge and blood to regenerate like the spring and not to remain frozen underground.

On the drought ridden Eastern Colorado Plains, one tradition is the time-honored, Western mythic image of cattle ranching. It is not questioned, but handed down to each generation in both expectation and image. An idealic myth supported by stock shows, rodeo, film, literature, advertisements, the cattleman's association, and the Beef Council. Yet cattle are a poor choice for poor soil. They tear the grass plant up whole by the roots instead of bison that nibble the top part of the plant and move on. Bison are also hardier and better adapted to the Great Plains than cattle because it is where they evolved. Without delving further into a scientific animal husbandry discussion, there are many sides to this senex and puer debate. Additionally, some on the side of the American bison would go further and suggest the reinstatement of a "Buffalo Commons." Some would call this a puer utopian dream, but the point here is the change (for prairie sustainability) is much needed and that our senex ideas of property and ownership need substantial modification to include all parts of the ecological and economic systems.

Perhaps as Hillman (2005) suggested we are in need of the "beady snake-eyes of Mercurius" to take advantage of seeing the necessity of opposites. While we are aware of the unsustainability of most of our wide-scale agricultural practices, we have a window of opportunity to see the between space. Hillman called this the "mercurial space" that allows a chance for *kairos*. This is a small space "where grand visions do not fit. By seeing with the beady snake-eyes of Mercurius, we make possible the appearance of Mercurius and of a hermetic significance in any situation. Puer consciousness may indeed act as psychopompos" (p. 109).

The tragedy that has led to the Dust Bowl, to short and tall grass prairie habitat loss, and to human population decline in these rural areas, has stemmed in part from a lack of ecological understanding and to what Hardin (1968) called in his essay, "The Tragedy of the Commons." In this essay, Hardin explored the dynamic that happens when an area of land (or other common holding) is used by many but which no one person owns responsibility. In the example of cattle ranching, which occurs on the public lands owned the United States Government and managed by the Bureau of Land Management, a single rancher may not be concerned about adding more cattle for grazing because that one rancher does not bear the cost burden of maintaining that grazing land. This is true also for other ranchers that have access use to the same land (by permits.) Therefore, singly no one rancher bears the cost, but they each benefit. But the land "in common" does bear the cost, and overall, all the ranchers eventually suffer the degradation of the land.

Hardin's essay was a major impetus for the move to privatize lands held in the public trust because it was believed to show that private land owners would take better care of their property. Freyfogle (2002) however, argued that by privatizing these large tracts of land, they would be broken up and fenced into small sections, and that this would lead to a "Tragedy of Fragmentation." Freyfogle's thesis (if you bracket out the impact of erecting more fencing and barriers to nature's ebb and flow of migration, habitat, and herd size) is that the problem is one of "dividing land into smaller units of governance in the situation where a government body has power to control land uses." Such greater governmental power is needed to oversee such larger landscape issues such as urban sprawl and habitat protection that cannot be managed by individual owners. He sums up his argument by seeing through, or in Hillman's term, psychologizing the situation:

> Fragmentation is a common byproduct of individualism and a love of individual liberty, and the United States embraces liberty and individualism more zealously than any other country in the world. But the nation has got itself into a bind. We need to back up a bit, drawing upon alternative strands in our cultural heritage, strands that honor cooperation rather than competition, that look to the benefits of shared action rather than

rugged individualism, that see the benefits to all in promoting, not our individual wants alone, but also jointly developed visions of the common good. (2002)

Fragmentation is an apt word for what Hillman (1975) deems falling apart, or *pathologizing*. Pathologizing is "the psyche's autonomous ability to create illness, morbidity, disorder, abnormality, and suffering in any aspect of its behavior and to experience and imagine life through this deformed and afflicted perspective" (p. 57). The tragedy of the commons and of fragmentation can be thought of as a pathology of the land. Specifically, the rugged individualism of the American West, Manifest Destiny, and progress have taken little care or concern for the earth or its indigenous peoples and the deep suffering is apparent in both.

The Myth

"The deepest nature of man, the secret of his soul as revealed by the modern metaphysic, is that he seeks to reach out beyond himself; knowing that negativity—death—is finite, he refuses to accept it. Behind the chiliasm of modern man is the megalomania of self-infinitization. In consequence, the modern hubris is refusal to accept limits."
—Daniel Bell, qtd. in, Kassiola, 2003

At the heart of the concept of fences and property is the myth that we can own the earth in any manner. This human-centered belief actions our laws, behaviors, psychology, religion, and our idea of soul. Hillman (1975) claimed that we are in psyche and the psyche is not in us. This thought is at the center of his move of *dehumanizing* or soul-making. With this idea, Hillman says we should ask "*Who?* and *What?* rather than *How?* and *Why?*" (p. 169) The "how" and "why" questions come from a science fantasy of psychology that relies on objectivity, technology, verification, and measurement. Hillman argues that the psyche or soul instead functions, or prefers root metaphors and its own operational myths. If we consider the *who* and *what* of property ownership and fencing, we can see that it is in part a refusal to accept limits. We buy up land and put up fences to limit other's access to what is "ours" but yet we unconsciously refuse the earth to limit us in return. We *take* ownership. We assume that what is "there for the taking" is ours by some fundamental right that only takes into consideration one factor; that of the human individual need.

Our fear of limits, of the final limit of death, brings us to the doors of science. In order to avoid limitations we give everything a name, a *how*, and a *why*. We measure, classify, and order, and use our technology to increase capacity, to increase yields, to gain the upper hand against the tyranny of nature and death which we cannot control. Our fear of limits and loss of control is the *who* and the *what* of our owning, our consumption, our stock piling, our fences, our guns.

This intense focus on the *who* and *what* as *ours* is a monotheistic concept that is based on the needs of the one; ourselves. In this one space, there can be no consideration for the future ones, for the past ones, let alone for those *Other* ones. Hillman's moves of psychologizing, personifying, pathologizing, and dehumanizing, is a move toward a polytheistic understanding that accounts for soul-making in a wider and deeper earth that embraces psyche inherent everywhere no matter the boundaries.

References

Abraham, L. (1998). *A dictionary of alchemical imagery.*
Cambridge, UK: Cambridge University Press.

Freyfogle, E. (2002). The Tragedy of Fragmentation.
Environmental Law Reporter, 32 (11).

Hardin, G. (1968). The Tragedy of the Commons. *Science,*
162 (3859), pp. 1243–1248.

Hillman, J. (1971). Psychology: Monotheistic or
polytheistic? *Spring,* 193-208.

Hillman, J. (1975). *Revisioning psychology.* San Francisco,
CA: Harper.

Hillman, J. (2005). An aspect of the historical and
psychological present. In G. Slater (Ed.), *Senex and*
puer (pp. 30-70). Putnam, CT: Spring Publications.

Hillman, J. (2005). Notes on opportunism. In G. Slater (Ed.), *Senex and puer* (pp. 96-112). Putnam, CT: Spring Publications.

Kassiola, J. J. (2003). *Explorations in environmental political theory: Thinking about what we value.* New York, NY: M. E. Sharpe.

Klein, C. A., Cheever, F., & Birdsong, B. C. (2005). *Natural resouces law: a place-based book of problems and cases.* New York, NY: Aspen Publishers.

McLaughlin, A. (2003). Industrialism and deep ecology. In J. J. Kassiola, *Explorations in environmental political theory: Thinking about what we value* (pp. 104-127). New York: M. E. Sharpe.

Slater, G. (2005). Introduction. In J. Hillman, & G. Slater (Ed.), *Senex and puer* (pp. VIV - XXVII). Putnam, CT: Spring Publications.

www.ingramcontent.com/pod-product-compliance
Lightning Source LLC
Chambersburg PA
CBHW071359310526
45790CB00019B/1651